Hit the Hat!

Written by Rachel Russ

Collins

Kat gets a kit.

It is a rock set.

Rick has a go.

Rick taps the tom tom.

Dan gets a rod.

Dan hits the hat.

hat

Cam has a red pan.

Cam raps the pan.

Meg and Mum tap it.

Meg and Mum pat it.

Tap, hit, rap, pat.

It is a din!

13

14

After reading

Letters and Sounds: Phase 2

Word count: 54

Focus phonemes: /r/ /h/

Common exception words: is, has, go, the, and

Curriculum links: Expressive Arts and Design: Exploring and using media and materials

Early learning goals: Reading: read and understand simple sentences; use phonic knowledge to decode regular words and read them aloud accurately; read some common irregular words; demonstrate understanding when talking with others about what they have read

Developing fluency

- Read the text to your child, modelling fluency and expression.
- Encourage your child to sound talk and then blend the words, e.g. r/o/d **rod**, h/a/t **hat**. It may help to point to each sound as your child reads.
- Reread each sentence to develop fluent reading with your child.

Phonic practice

- Ask your child to sound talk and blend each of the following words: r/e/d r/o/d r/a/p
- Look at the "I spy sounds" pages (14 and 15). Discuss the picture with your child. Can they find items/ examples of words containing the /r/ and /h/ sounds? (*recorder, rooster, drum, rabbit, radio, reading, racing car, hoop, house, hippo*)

Extending vocabulary

- Ask your child:
  - The children on page 13 are making a **din**. What words can you use to describe the noise drums make? (e.g. *bang, boom, thud, crash, clang, clatter*)
  - Look in the book. What words can you find that mean "hit"? (*tap, pat, rap*) Can you think of any others? (e.g. *bang, knock*)